Other Books by Sheila Bender

Behind Us the Way Grows Wider,
Collected Poems 1980 – 2013

Creative Writing DeMYSTiFieD

Keeping a Journal You Love

Love from the Coastal Route,
Selected Poems

Near the Light, Poems

A New Theology:
Turning to Poetry in a Time of Grief

Perfect Phrases for College Application Essays

Sorrow's Words: Writing Exercises to Heal Grief

Sustenance, New and Selected Poems

The Writer's Journal:
40 Writers and Their Journals

Writing in a Convertible with the Top Down,
co-authored with Christi Glover

Writing Personal Essays:
Shaping and Sharing Your Life Experiences

Writing Personal Poetry:
Creating Poems from Your Life Experiences

A Year in the Life:
Journaling for Self-Discovery

SINCE THEN
POEMS AND SHORT PROSE

Ex Ophidia Press

Praise for Sheila Bender

As Sheila Bender writes, "Sorrow is your guardian. She's got/ your back." For anyone who has experienced the loss of a loved one, or is anticipating such a loss (which means everyone!), this book also serves as a "guardian" for our grief. Bender has our back as we navigate this rocky and unmapped terrain. I read this book in one sitting, gratitude welling along with my tears.

— Brenda Miller, *A Braided Heart: Essays on Writing and Form*

A tender meditation on loss, fierce with grace, and alive with love. Bender's poetry grips us immediately, each poem filled with enormous beauty, ache and wisdom, each poem holding us tight until the last line: "holding them dear even as I must let them go."

— Anna Quinn, *The Night Child*

Ms. Sheila Bender's second book on the poetic restoration of her son's traumatic death decades ago will provide a written template for re-establishing transcendence over tragedy. It follows the trajectory of living with the joy and sorrow that exists — at once old and ever new in us after loss(s).

— Ted Rynearson MD, Virginia Mason Grief Services,
   Seattle, Washington

In her moving new collection, *Since Then: Poems and Short Prose,* grief and sorrow are Sheila Bender's constant companions. In fact, what she has written could be read as a textbook, or guidebook, on how to live after an incalculable loss.

Each of the book's four sections begins with a letter to the poet's son, Seth, whose accidental death years earlier has left an immense vacancy that can only be filled by opening a direct line of communication. Bender addresses her dead son both in these letters and the poems that follow. They're heartbreaking to read.

But that's not the full story. The poems in this collection reveal a life made rich equally by remembrance and by being in the present moment. The poems touch on travel, reflections from childhood, the restorative power of gardening and, in one poem, on the curious mating habits of hummingbirds. Bender's book teaches us that joy and wonder are still possible, even when grief is never far, as close as in the next room, as near at hand as these evocative, haunting, life-affirming pages.

— Ed Harkness, author of *The Law of the Unforeseen*

In *Since Then,* author, poet, and teacher Sheila Bender has created an artful and complex cartography of loss with a series of poems, letters, and daily witnessing. She searches for "the handholds and footholds" in "grief's rock wall" to climb toward the brightness of understanding that a mother "can grieve her son and at the same time continue with his life alongside hers, allow colors and sensations that keep him alive." *Since Then* allows readers to experience healing's job, which is to help the bereaved find gratitude for all they still have even as they hold the knowledge of what has been lost.

— Gayle Kaune MSW, LICSW, author of *All the Birds Awake, Still Life in the Physical World,* and *Noise from Stars*

In her new book, *Since Then,* Sheila Bender writes of her life since the loss of her beloved son, a young man who died on the cusp of his own life, now twenty-one years ago. Bender is a writer and a teacher, she is a wife, mother, grandmother, friend, there is a fullness to her life, much to observe and cherish. But such a loss as she suffered does not fade. Reading Sheila Bender's *Since Then,* we come to understand that surrendering to grief does not diminish life, but serves to deepen it. This is a beautiful book. I am the wiser and the richer for having read it.

— Abigail Thomas, *What Comes Next* and *How to Like It*

"I read time now like a book," Sheila Bender says, "this life / broken into before and after." Alternately heartbreaking and redemptive, the poems in this radiant collection teach us how to live with incalculable loss—the death of one's child — and then go on, "climbing toward the brightness we shared." Artfully structured, each section of the book introduced by letters to her son, these intimate and consoling poems are a record of alert and tender noticing, of life deeply lived and celebrated, and of the hard-won knowledge that "sorrow doesn't have to be an unending pall but a source of deep loving." Isn't this why we read poetry? *Since Then* will go on the shelf of books I turn to for succor and delight, for help finding the way forward with grief into "the only present possible," alive and infused with wonder. The book is a gift to the world.

— Alison Townsend, Emerita Professor English, author of *Persephone in America* and *The Blue Dress*

Sheila Bender's *Since Then: Poems and Short Prose* begins with a letter that asks the question, "Dear Seth, Did I ever tell you..." The first poem ends with "Sorrow is your guardian...to help you choreograph / what is ferocious and freshly wild." The memoir is about remembering the life and death of her son Seth, as well as chronically the life she has made for herself and her family in the years since. She travels within and outside herself in places close to home — Discovery Bay, her garden, writing, husband, and daughter's family in the Pacific Northwest — as well as far away — the North Sea, the Baltic, Denmark, and sand dunes. She deftly weaves the specifics of times and places that both ground us in the day-to-day — turtles, barn-red ledges, and umbrellas — and reminds us that *this* life of ours is one of contradiction, / a boat drifting around an anchor. Yet, she also steps out into new experiences and into acceptance. Sheila Bender's book is like looking through a windowpane from both sides — on grief as well as joy.

— Susan Landgraf

Sheila Bender's new volume *Since Then* is a remarkable poetic account of the way a human being can transform mortal heartbreak into a sustaining love of the world. Sonically lush, elegantly imaginative, and formally diverse, the poems act as direct and indirect milestones in the life of a mother looking back on the life of a son who died decades ago. Pushing courageously beyond the keening of maternal pain, they depict her path forward into a radical appreciation of the present moment. Guided by four epistolary prose poems addressed to her son, the book is alive with both her striking self-examining lyrics about him as well as more outward-looking poems about the grace of our natural environment and the enhancing particularity of things. For me, the overarching achievement of *Since Then* is its rendering the way in which grief can — over time — be infused with a kind of receptive, awe-ready sentience that holds to memory while accepting finality. As she says in "Now," the book's deeply moving final poem, she has come to "savor…who [her son] will always be." Readers who commit to Sheila Bender's profoundly personal and philosophical verse exploration will find that this collection is near epic in its scope and project.

— Kevin Clark, author of *The Consecrations*

Sheila Bender's evocative, poignant, and complementary prose and poetry together create a tender and luminous meditation on the complex nature of grief in all its myriad manifestations. Bender's powerful writing is both particular and universal: Readers will easily identify with her heartfelt emotional and literary journeys, as well as with her authenticity and courage. Her eloquent work is imbued with a tremendous generosity of spirit toward her readers, her loved ones, and herself.

— Janice Eidus, author of T*he War of the Rosens* and
   The Last Jewish Virgin

SINCE THEN
POEMS AND SHORT PROSE

Sheila Bender

Ex Ophidia Press
2022

Design: Jim Jones
Production: Marcia Breece
Cover photo: Emily Menon Bender

Ex Ophidia Press
17037 10th Avenue NE
Shoreline, Washington 98155

exophidiapress.org

ISBN: 978-1-7373851-3-4

For those I miss most

CONTENTS

One

Two

Three

Four

SINCE THEN
POEMS AND SHORT PROSE

When where's
the Word dawning, tell me, if not with Night
in its riverbed of tears,
Night that shows plunging suns the sown seed
over and over again?
— Paul Celan

One

Absence is a house so vast that inside you will pass through its walls and hang pictures on the air.
— Pablo Neruda

Dear Seth,

Did I ever tell you how I loved seeing your arm hooked up and around the top of a page as you wrote for your school assignments? How I loved your neat and regular left-handed printing? How I wondered at your letters so regularly spaced, their height so even? How handsome you had gotten, how deep your voice, how dreamy your blue, blue eyes, how lovely your curls and the strength in your hands?

I like remembering when you and your Steppie, as you called Kurt, supported me in making my dream come true — to write by water, a bay called Discovery. The joy of Kurt helping me pick out the building lot. The excitement when at seventeen you asked to design the house. Do you remember saying as a little boy that you would build me a house on wheels and drive me around and around so I could write?

I am sure, though, that you remember my caution, "Seth, I don't know if we can afford to build the house you design."

"Mom, I have to interview you and Kurt about what you each want in a house, and we'll see."

"I'd like three bedrooms and three bathrooms," I told you, thinking about wanting others to be comfortable on visits.

"I'd like room for a pool table in the basement," Kurt said, imagining his guests.

"Mom, your budget allows for two bedrooms and two baths with showers. Kurt, I'll find out how much a basement raises the cost of the project. But I'm not hopeful."

It's outlandish and funny looking back that we would ask for so much. Wearing your rust-colored button-down cotton shirt rolled to the elbow, you hooked your left arm over the notebook you brought to our meeting, the very same way you would over the paper on your drafting table when you designed the project we could afford. You seemed to know what you were doing right from the get-go.

On the anniversary of your birth, I look (as I often do since your death) at a photograph of you at five wearing a yellow hardhat you had selected as your prop for the kindergarten class photo. I look at the corners in this house you designed, the wooden trim, the windows as plentiful as the building permit allowed. I laugh when I look at the hardwood floors — worried about the budget, I was thinking of foregoing them. It was time for you to present your design as a high school project and when you came home that day, you told me the whole class voted not to cut the hardwood floors. Peer pressure for sure but different peers, I thought.

All this summer, I have entertained guests from Seattle, Jacksonville, Cleveland, Bellingham, and Los Angeles, offered luncheons and dinners under the great room's skylights knowing that fall and the excruciating calendar of missing would come. Your birthday, then Thanksgiving which marks the last visit you made to see us, December 27 the day of your accident, December 28 the day we agreed to take you off life support, January 2 the synagogue services before we scattered your ashes.

Now, as the mourning season begins again, I imagine a wife and children paddling with you along the shores of Discovery Bay in the crafted wooden kayaks you dreamed of showing your children how to build.

With all my love (always!),

Mom

In the Room of Mourning

After All Our Sorrows,
a painting by Nancy Van Allen

Sorrow is your guardian. She's got
your back, watches as you sit
on grief's hard bench
under a ceiling so high
warm air cannot
encircle you

or fill
the space where
memories are lost.
She'll spin away sometimes,
then return to help you choreograph
what is ferocious and freshly wild.

Undeniable Haunting

The thin blond-haired boy
you knew who died of a heart attack
at recess, teachers cradling his head.

The high school girl killed by the downhill
momentum of a truck's heavy tire
dislodged from its lugs.

The photograph of sixteen-year-old you at a party
smiling alongside a cherished family friend
and a cousin not yet in kindergarten,

both of them dead soon after it was taken.
The law of three meant you would be next,
so you feared movie dates with your boyfriend,

sure the chains holding the theater's chandelier
would snap while you stared at the ceiling
and you'd meet death under shards of glass.

Even after years of not dying you felt fated,
believed tragedy would strike, and it did, killing
your son on a Colorado mountaintop.

No risk too small now to trigger you
for calamity, a shoe in the middle of a hallway,
water glass too close to a table's edge.

The smallest scratch on a table, the lightest
scuff on the floor, faint stain on a shirt,
an undeniable haunting.

Reload

I load the dishwasher, washing machine, pantry
while Grief sweeps shards of a shattered moon.

I go for a drive into sunlight, and she scrambles
into the passenger seat beside me.

Once my son drank milk from a half gallon
carton before my eyes.

Once he picked out a dining room fixture
and installed light for us. Once he caulked our sink.

Once we were short of breath together in the Rockies.
and once we rode mountain bikes up curbs.

Once he said his sister's reading made him bored
and then he went to college and began to enjoy books.

Grief does not smile with me. She listens to every
wishful breath in and tearful one out.

My Mother Has Gone to China

Her friend said she was taking a tour and asked
my mother to pack her things and go.
(Stutter buzz of the clasps on Father's brown briefcase.)

Is she watching cigarette-scented men play mahjong,
the clicking of tiles muting the pain of his death?
(Smoke of my father's Pall Malls drifting out his car window.)

Is my mother touching the Great Wall?
(Families of china animals he brought home
from business trips housed in our fruitwood breakfront.)

Is she eating wok-fried vegetables and crisp noodles?
(At a Chinese restaurant he sang, "I'm a bubble, I'm a bubble,"
to cheer me into thinking I could be popular.)

Is my mother wearing shower thongs?
(White plastic tube in his belly
when he could no longer swallow.)

Is she buying silk scarves and jackets?
(On my Wisconsin campus when wind chill
created temps of minus sixty, he refused a hat, relented
     at earmuffs.)

Is she admiring Ming Dynasty furniture?
(His parents wouldn't bequeath him their replicas.
He slammed his car door so hard, the rest of us rocked
     as if on an ocean.)

Is she riding in a rickshaw?
(He taught me to cha-cha and jitterbug,
to make turns when the music was right.)

In dreams my father slicks back the hair he imagines
still there on his bald head.
(He told me to take care of my mother.)

Is my mother looking for jade?
(In my dreams, pet turtles he brought us
escape again behind our apartment's hot stove.)

How to Grieve Your Father

Sit on the bench donated in your son's name.
He died six months before your father died from Parkinson's.

The bench invites you to reflect as the sun rises over the bay.
Your son was sunrise, your father sunset.

Your cousin told you your father said
it should have been him.

Look at dawn lighting the sky with pink and yellow,
colors of long-ago dolls' clothes.

Remember.

Your father taught you to declutter the room you
        shared with your sister.

Do you need this? And this? Where does this belong?
Those things out of place, those things with no place,
like your grief over your father's passing.

Think of the day you sat on a toilet lid watching him shave.
Suddenly the building's sewer backed up. He fled to work
telling your mother to rise from bed and call a plumber.

Know you cannot clean or declutter grief. Know you may
        want to walk
away from its mess because one memory begets others,
like objects you would put in a treasure box
if you had one and knew where it belonged.

Forecast

Asphalt of the plowed and snow-edged road
resembles a seatbelt over a white parka,
a tie against a dress shirt.

Nettle vines along my fence have lost
their disguise as a snow drift;
only small white caps top their green mounds.

Unrobed, pine trees hold pom-poms
at the end of their green-sleeved arms, like cheerleaders
raising spirits between two storms.

In the Writing Workshop

A calendar cover pinned to the far wall proclaims
　　Divine Comedy,
pictures a ghost or an angel, maybe a priest in white robes;
who can tell from where I sit?

Next to the cover, a page of April's dates tilts right
with a graphic of boots wrapped in low fog.
Do I make out a starry sky above?

*

Time is not linear, they say,
though our lives mostly are.

*

If I reach into the jumble of days,
will coffee still drip into the red pot? My feet
still touch this classroom's brand-new floor?

Who Lives on the Other Side

Who lives on the other side of the pond
in the house I see through a corkscrew willow?

Who lives on the other side of years
since I owned a house with a corkscrew willow,

since I sold its branches once a year to one florist
a block around the corner, then two more down the street,

since I was raising children who loved two kittens,
one Seth called Midnight, the other Emily's Melissa,

since Midnight was stolen from our yard and Seth
absorbed his loss and his sister's good fortune,

since a coyote destroyed the quails he kept in a backyard
pen, only grey feathers left,

since Seth was stolen from us by the icy slopes of
Breckenridge one winter's snowboarding run?

Who lives on the other side of my grief, regular as sunset,
hungry as deer in early spring nibbling

buds on the drooping branches of that corkscrew willow?
I stand before a windbreak of poplar trees

viewing a house on the other shore as if whoever
lives there will open its quiet door.

Two

. . . [T]he bad news is that you never completely get over the loss of your beloved. But this is also the good news. They live forever in your broken heart that doesn't seal back up. And you come through. It's like having a broken leg that never heals perfectly — that still hurts when the weather gets cold, but you learn to dance with the limp.

— Anne Lamott

Dear Seth,

Your grandmother says that often at night, she has a vision of you and your grandfather sitting on a ledge above her talking. When I ask what you are saying to one another, she says she doesn't know.

Why on a ledge?

The word sticks with me, and I look it up today, the tenth anniversary of your accident, in the *Merriam-Webster* online dictionary. This would not surprise you, since you know I am a believer that words hold wisdom in their definitions and etymologies. It wouldn't surprise you, either, that I can't stop myself from searching and go to Dictionary.com and to the *Online Etymology Dictionary*.

What the *Merriam-Webster* tells me:

1. a raised or projecting edge or molding intended to protect or check; a window ledge
2. an underwater ridge or reef especially near the shore
3. rock that is solid or continuous enough to form ledges: bedrock as in "the field was full of ledge"

I look out the large windows of *your* house, Discovery Bay shimmering over the bluff. The fir trim of the windowsills has darkened now with age into a honey red-orange. I can see the south wall of the house's exterior, the window ledges outside, which remain painted the same dark barn red as when the house was built. When it was time to repaint, Kurt and I couldn't part with any of the details we had chosen with you, who designed this house even before you were formally on your way to becoming an architect.

I think about the quiet distinction between the barn-red ledges and the original natural cedar color of the shingles on the house's exterior. They've weathered gray over the last years. *I know, I know, come spring and dry weather, we must have*

19

them sealed. I know, yes, we cannot do the power washing too
many times without risking the strength of the shingles. I heed
the caution I imagine in your voice letting me know, as always,
what I must be sure to take care of. I am certain only something
thin as a windowpane separates your world and mine.

I look to the bay you loved exploring. Kurt and I sat once
with a visiting cousin on a ledge of beached driftwood as you
pulled your well-crafted kayak ashore and urged the rest of
us to take her out for a paddle. And I remember the day your
fiancée Kristen paddled out in that boat to release your ashes,
the story, too, of your marriage proposal to her on your dad's
boat docked for the night in Port Townsend Bay where the two
of you had sailed from Seattle. Your grandmother kept secret
that you had asked her for the ring she promised you, your great
grandmother's ring, to slip onto Kristen's finger. You were ready
for that other journey, for the children you would have together,
ready to teach them to love the woods and the water.

Each new year since you left is a ledge for me on grief's
rock wall. I look for the handholds and footholds that will
allow me to climb toward the brightness we shared. Your sister's
growing sons, who sleep when they are here on a trundle
bed in the room you designed as my study, Kristen's new life
with a husband and family, and a decade of caring for your
grandmother have helped me learn that sorrow doesn't have to
be an unending pall, but a source of deep loving.

Kurt keeps a photograph of you on his office wall. You are
in Central California, poring over blueprints laid out on the
ground, talking with your project partners about the next step
in building a covered bus shelter you want for field hands who
labor all day under hot sun, then must wait in the same hot sun
for their bus home. As I sit looking out *your* windows watching
my bay, I think of your spirit, solid and continuous, bedrock I
hold inside of me. I know your kindness is in the asparagus I

will steam for dinner, in the cabbage of the simmering healing soup I make, in the seeds I will plant again this spring in our ever-expanding vegetable garden.

For now, I sit in a chair, its legs I have learned, supported by what carpenters call a ledge, and I read more of the word's etymology.

To lay hands on

To lay eggs

To allege

I, who would lay my hands on your shoulders knowing you were always hatching a new adventure, look up "allege" and find a definition I wasn't aware of: "To alleviate; to lighten, as a burden or a trouble."

As the year turns and we go on without you, I sit wondering what you are saying in your grandmother's vision.

Of course, I would love for you to speak to me in a dream or a vision of my own.

With love always,

Mom

My Writing Partner's Words to Me in Class

I have to go. I have to leave. I'm sorry;
if I don't, my legs will stiffen.

I don't know why. I don't know what it is,
but if I sit beyond an hour, I'll stumble when I get up.

Where there are no sidewalks, I put my feet
on the road's white line and concentrate

to walk the stiffness out but sometimes
it makes it worse.

At the theater I step on toes.
"Oops, sorry."

"We step on them, too,"
the people joke.

Now it will be Netflix, not theaters,
taking stairs slow, down harder than up.

Cruising at 40,000 Feet on Emirates Airlines

Silverware wrapped in a linen napkin I'll place on my lap,
attendants with offers of juices, apple and orange,
even *aloo* for breakfast if I want it. And I do.

With the tray table tucked close to my stomach, I savor
sauteed spinach, potatoes, cauliflower, and peas,
taste of earth between where I was and where I am going.

Writing Retreat, Denmark

At first,
I listen for pockets
of my own language.

Gradually,
I'm happy without
distractions

only
rain and wind
and sea buckthorn.

Then,
at a bakery
for coffee and a roll

jangle
of unfamiliar coins
landing on a polished counter.

Solo at a Ferry Dock

A ladybug on my wrist crawls
part way up my purple sleeve
then transits across my waist,
reaches the strap of my travel bag
and waits to see where we
are going, just like me.

Thinking about Time
at the Case of Old Watches

At the Den Gamle By Museum,
Aarhus, Denmark

What was then?
What is now?
What is after
and what before?

What is since
and what belated?
What was yesterday?
and what awhile?

What is when
and what is always?
For what tomorrow?

Just after Rain, I Finally Smile

And the sun is out enough to make
the sparkle of drops on rose petals
surprise me like the quartz stones
I find on beach walks.

And the round hips beneath the flowers!
May they grow ample, each under
their own court jester's cap.

In My Attic Room in Aarhus, Denmark

I store my life in four cubbies, make a skinny
em-dash of clothes along one wall.

I sleep well under the slanted ceiling,
stand upright only in the room's center.

The Danes pride themselves on being
the world's most balanced people.

Haiku on a Rainy Afternoon

After sudden storms
blue skies, amusing white clouds,
but sad leaves still fall

With My Grandsons,
Tivoli Friheden, Aarhus Rainstorm

Only one coat for three
We share it like an awning
The flowers' wet smiles

Solo Day Senryu

Backpack in Aarhus
with everything I need
My hands wide open

Pantoum from Northern Jutland

For Emily and Vijay, who took me there

At the top of Jutland, where two seas meet,
my daughter and her family and I stand
with one of our feet in each of the seas
to see which of the two is the coldest.

My daughter and her family and I
take our time before we put in our votes
about which of the two is the coldest;
we know it is a very close match.

We take our time before we put in our votes;
my oldest grandson leans toward the Baltic.
Though the two are a very close match,
more sun seems to polish the North Sea's ripples.

My oldest grandson sticks with the Baltic;
as a baby he flinched in slight breezes.
The sun warms the shallower ripples,
but I vote just as he does.

As a baby he flinched in breezes by windows;
I look at the smile made by the swirls of the waves
and I vote now as he does,
awed by his height, how he's taller than I am.

I look at the smile made by the swirls of the waves.
How the two seas seem a slit in a skirt
and my grandson is taller than I am;
my daughter says not a slit, but a zipper.

I see the two seas as a slit in a skirt
while I stand in the sand in the small space between.
My daughter says not a parting, a zipper,
three generations fastened by waves in the water.

While I stand in the sand in the small space between,
my daughter proclaims not a parting, a zipper.
three generations fastened by waves and by water.
And I stand in the sand smiling among them.

Out Wandering, Aarhus, Denmark

When the wind blusters behind me and the hair
at the back of my head rushes toward my face,
I imagine a white line of scalp revealed,
like this sandy path lined by sea buckthorn —
and I don't think of the coming storm.

I Need a Fifteen-Year Supply
of Beer and Toilet Paper, a Roundel

With words from a Steve Jackson game

I'm playing the game *Munchkin Apocalypse*
with my two strategic grandsons.
I scratch my head and purse my lips;
I'm not like them; this game's complications are no fun.

The cards, especially the treasure ones, make them laugh a ton:
Collapsible Toothbrush, Dehydrated Water, Arm-y Surplus.
Apparently, allowed three human hands, how lucky
    you've become.

There are social circles, too: Kid, Blogger, Militia and Scientist,
cards with tips, bonuses, bounties, and premiums,
monsters to outrun. Things called Biblical Seals send you
    on scary trips.
I am not like these boys. These complications are no fun!

Novel

The one I'd write starts with a woman counting
her days in paper coffee filters and the number of times
she pours boiled water over the two rounded
scoops she fills them with.

One day she might add slips from Chinese fortune cookies
collected for years, and douse them, too,
in the liquid that drips into her heavy
ceramic coffee mug.

For now, though, I imagine she watches cars travel down the hill
beyond her front door, relishes her garden's red penstemon,
the white drifts of Shasta daisies that remind her
of sand dunes and of winter.

December 27

This is the day my earth spins relentlessly toward,
when I go to sleep in sadness, the day we lost you
on an icy mountain we never thought about
until then and now always in this life
broken into before and after.

On this day we watch the winter sun
rise from sea level, hoping for a hawk circling
as on so many anniversaries reminding us
of your love for these Northwest woods and water,
the children you would have loved, how we
would have loved them too. It is good to conjure you.

Three

Grief changes shape, but it never ends.
— Keanu Reeves

December Night, 2015

Dear Seth,

I wake suddenly at two AM and try my best to stay still, but I am restless. I slip out of bed careful not to wake Kurt as I walk through the dark hallway to our living room. In the moonlight that comes in from our front windows, I see the Costco million-packs of paper towels and tissues sitting on our couch, the economy size box of kitchen trash bags on the seat of my favorite chair. Jars of almond butter and bottles of maple syrup the length of the kitchen counter, cellophane bags of more staples nestled in cloth grocery bags on the floor. We plan each excursion to be one we don't often repeat.

Cleaning up in our little house now will wake Kurt, so I settle into my second-choice chair and begin to think about things out of place.

I think about my instigation of bathroom remodels during the summer, how with nowhere to store materials, the contractor took over one of our two bedrooms, how we had to empty a tall armoire he needed to move. I see again the colorful cloth of our lives residing on the living room couch in a pile Kurt called our Turkish bazaar, since we'd been to Istanbul that May and images of the colorful city remained vivid. All of June, July, August and September, our front door was open, men tearing down walls, wiring for new spaces, and laying down tile, needing ventilation and easy access in and out. Flies flew in widening circles. When Kurt had an emergency appendectomy and a week later was released from the hospital, we began sleeping in our office, Kurt in a reclining chair to keep him from tossing and turning and disrupting the incision and me on a sofa bed. We called to one another, "Good night, Baby, sleep tight," "Do you need anything?" "Yes, maybe some water."

During the months of our things and ourselves out of place — bags of items from vanity drawers in a corner by my dresser, maple doors lining the wall behind Kurt's dresser, of summer plans cancelled as Kurt recovered — I grew restless

41

about restoring order. I weeded through ill-fitting old jeans and shirts, made trips to Goodwill, sorted through forgotten keys, discarded the ones that opened none of our doors.

Once the contractors finished, we dusted and vacuumed and vacuumed and dusted, at five feet tall, my vision directed to the floors and tables, and at six foot three, Kurt's efforts concentrated on the tops of our cabinets and high shelves.

Kurt has named the new shower the Carnegie shower because its acoustics for singing are the best he's ever experienced in a bathroom. The guest bathroom has room for a tub and an entrance more discreet than the original. But every time I walk to that new entrance, retrace a walkway different than the one you designed for our built-on-a-tight-budget home, I feel what is missing, what will never be the same. I relive your sudden death, feel the bittersweetness of our lives going on. For years, I needed everything as it was to feel you, my boy, with me.

"Seth would like what you did very much," your grandmother soothed. She knew how deep my wish all these months to have consulted with you about the changes to "your" house.

It was a dream that awoke me tonight. In it, I walked from bedroom to living room. Outside the window, a large coyote sat comfortably in our deck rocking chair looking over the shrubbery in our front yard. As I approached the window glass, the animal loped into the garden. I turned from the glass, and he came back, taking his comfortable seat. When I google information on coyotes, I learn the animal can survive in the desert, on the beach, in the forest and mountains, becoming a part of environments that change over time. One website emphasizes that the coyote symbolizes the need to focus on what you are going to do with what you have.

I remember asking you for help in planning the landscaping after the house was built. You told me that part of our project was up to me. Perhaps the dream coyote came to remind me that I am grateful for this house you designed, grateful to have been able to update it, grateful for Kurt's quick recovery, and grateful for the coyote who drew me from sleep to stillness among the clutter of emotions I need to live with, taking them out, sometimes putting them away.

With love and gratitude to you forever,

Mom

Visiting the Old Neighborhood in Winter, a Villanelle

The marriage, the move, my divorce,
lovers come and gone, the children grown.
Now on familiar streets of joy and tears I walk alone.

Some bungalows and Tudors in renovation,
others with lamp-lit windows where memories are sown;
marriage, the move, my separation.

I do not shed nostalgia, or weep at days
gone by. My memories are honed.
These familiar streets hold joys and tearful ways.

I am the grandmother now at concerts and at sports;
I treasure who and what I've loved and lost and known,
the marriage, the move, my divorce.

The tree trunks raise the sidewalks here and there,
stout roots spreading and full of knots.
These streets hold years of joy and tears.

In the clarity of cold I see what it is I feared
and learned — that what we long for are resting spots,
my marriage, the move, even my divorce;
these streets I walk alone are made of joy and tears.

By a Window Overlooking a Ravine

I.
An *and,* a *that,* an *adjective*
remove themselves.
A fissure and my poem arrives.

II.
Poems sit in chairs at my table or nibble my cuffs
like hedgehogs clamoring for peaches or a week's
worth of crickets, carrots, and worms.

III.
My poems sail in the cold water of Discovery Bay.
They also capsize and drift, come ashore
like logs in a storm, beach themselves
because of the weather.

IV.
By a window overlooking a ravine,
with a view to the snow-covered mountains,
revision is in the air.
A line becomes a title.

My Face in the Mirror with Blue-Framed Glasses

Color of my aquamarine birthstone, of earrings
my mother gave me when I turned sixteen.
Behind the lenses of these spectacles,
blue eyes of my father, blue eyes my mother's
friends admired, eyes I wished boyfriends
might too, such beautiful blue eyes, the women said,
eyes my husband cannot remember the color of, strange
unless you know he is color blind but strange
all the same, this blue not the color of my birthstone
but of the sky my Pisces self looks to as she
dreams in the sea fewer days than I wish her to,
both of us looking up from the water, our eyes
wet and shining into the light.

Six Poets Paint Together at Jim's Studio

Around the table we each paint
within our nine by twelve portions of the long
paper, laughter showing up in waves
and birds, a fish, the sun.

Behind us, Jim's parrot chirps,
a shoe squeaks, the microwave's beep
signals food is done.

Writing in Jim's Art Studio

Cacti, aloe, sedum under the grow light,
the parrot quiet now in her castle of branches,
a half-empty pot of coffee on a hot plate.

Jim fingerpaints purple on the edges of an orange
sun, taps the handle of his brush to splatter
white spots, snow or a galaxy.

Play with Me

Neener neener neener
back to the jungle, Sheena

Slurp, burp, sought, caught
skip around a fort

Chimes, chiming
chiming chimes

Foxtrot
Jackie Grossbart?

Whoopsie daisy
cold, warm, and very hot

Dog shakes fur, stutters air
Cormorants sunning on a pier.

Amour, Amar

"I heard you were looking for me." His voice sparkles over the phone bringing me out of a deep sleep several time zones away from where he lives. The postcard has arrived at his mother's pied-à-terre in Manhattan.

"She wasn't going to tell me. She was afraid I'd gotten a girl in trouble and had a kid needing money to go to college."

At fifteen, my daughter is going to France with a Rotary Club high school exchange program, and she wondered if I ever found the Frenchman I looked for years ago when she was five and her father and I divorced. I'd sent printed postcards with a message in French to every Amar in the phone books of Nice and Paris, where I remembered his family had homes.

Eighteen years after we'd met at Laurel Lake Camp in New York State, both of us counselors then for twelve-year-olds, my logical daughter asks where I'd seen him last. And I remembered New York City. We'd met for a day to say goodbye before he returned to Paris for graduate school.

How had I forgotten that his mother, a professor at the Sorbonne, had a New York apartment he stayed in?

My daughter surprises me with Xeroxes of Amars in the library's Manhattan telephone directory.

Postcards with a message in English, postcards to only eleven people, and the sound of our voices now carries us back to that lake, red canoes, sleeping bags and bonfires, rainy days reading *Scientific American* on the bleachers of the camp gym, the words *Je t'aime, Je t'aime.*

Everyday Excitement

While the saleswoman snips the nylon thread that secures
a plastic bag of extra buttons for the newly
purchased shirt I plan on wearing out of the store,
I think
  button up,
    buttonholes, boutonnieres,
      circles of sliced
        shallots tonight
          popping in the frying pan.

Writing in the Second Person

Today you sit at the head of a long oak table,
four of them actually, pushed together, two golden,
one dark as mahogany, the last painted black, your students
three to a side, no one facing you from the end.

Do not look at the cracks between the tables
where your best words could escape. Do not look
at the three empty chairs, one red, one black, one green.
This table should not be a sentence that ends in ellipsis.

How the students write! And write!
You gave them a prompt to occupy their minds
so associations might become a torrent of words
to reveal something smarter than they knew they could be.

If you are lucky, you can help your students see and hear,
smell and taste the associations, understand the touch
        of their pens
to paper as salve. But only if you keep your attention
from the empty green chair, the red one, the black.

At the grocery store, you may meet those three enrolled
who didn't show up. They will apologize saying they
        weren't confident,
or company came or the kids got sick. Do not look
at the green chair, the black one, the red.

You think two of the chairs are like sentries guarding
        the third
and remember you hate the word sentries (and sentinel, too)
because what stands on the sides prevents passage,
        as if that could ever lead to good writing.

In the Edge of Shade from Two Umbrellas

I.
I gaze across Puget Sound to Seattle. The hum and buzz
    of a small plane
flies me back before jets and crowded skies to the summers
    of my NJ childhood
where I waited in the grass outside our garden apartment eager
    for my mother's
family to arrive from Brooklyn duplexes. In the Yiddish
    that clambered
from their Chevrolets and Buicks, I heard the snap
    of crunched berries.

II.
The rhythmic laps of incoming tide — swish of nylons
thigh against thigh, click of short heels on our 1960s
junior high gym floors, cheek to check, twisting
    and shouting;
if only the right one would notice me.

III.
This paper soggy with humidity feels like raw filo dough,
and I remember baklava, a trip to Greece, days I wrote
    with a pencil
under an olive tree. The word *Athena* and the way they said
    white cheese
bring breezes rustling my notebook's pages.

IV.
The writers who've beckoned me to teach this summer day
bow over their notebooks, pens gliding. Five minutes,
ten, then twenty. I will call time now, listen to where they
have been in this shade, where they may have
turned to the sunlight beyond.

Left

Handedness of my son
dead now eighteen years

Handedness of my mother
still here at ninety-four

My son's hand curved
over his drafting table like a crescent moon

In my mother's
the white handle of a magnifying glass for reading

Below my ring finger's knuckle
moon-white skin from the wedding band I wore.

To a Fiancé Who Fled Three Weeks before the Wedding Date

Words for my student who couldn't write to him

Have you tried to forget how you left so many stones unturned,
so much firewood stacked but never burned?

You invited me in.

Or should I say invited me out? Those claws my legs
evolved to become, that venom they can spout,

perhaps as accurately as giant Scolopendra
shoots from each of her appendages.

I'm writing to let you know
that whatever is next for you and next again,

I will always be in the mulch of all your beds,
as if a dozen legs were moving toward you in a wave of one.

Imprisoned in a self-barricading circle
of your — can I even call it love — I finally found myself.

Rule of thumb: don't ever handle a centipede.
Really. I mean it. Believe me, I am not writing for your apology.

Until today, I never thought to enter that drawer
I'd kept of your tee shirts to eat through each of them,

one by one. I'm done. No more cotton to cotton onto you.

I Scream

These poor children. I'm afraid to say this
and it hurts me to say this, but the evidence
is irrefutable, they have no soul.
                    — Ted Nugent on student
                       gun control advocates

I wonder if you mean that the soulful require
assault rifles to shred the flesh, bones
and organs of being human, leaving no shape or form,

if you think the soul of our country
lives in your steel barrels, cages for your heart?
I saw a ten-year-old demonstrator

holding a sign, "Am I next?" And where would
she die, among so many possibilities — stores, cafes,
schools, theaters, airports, malls, hotels, festivals, freeways?

I wonder what you find soulful about no need
for background checks, about carrying guns
in schools and in churches, about those eager to fire?

Ted Nugent, Ted Nugent, Ted Nugent,
I see your soul in the congressman's
mouth as he proclaims he'll shove a red hot

poker up a student gun protester's ass.
I scream. I scream at you from this page.
Do you ever wonder at your grace-starved world?

Written in the Ink

After Dinosaur *by Bruce Holland Rogers*

When Norman was thirteen, about to become a bar mitzvah, he threw his aunt's gift of an Italian inkwell out the upstairs window of his family's Brooklyn brownstone.

"You can't do that," his mother yelled, "How can you receive the Torah? You are stupid as soup!"

Since he was not soup, he thought he might be a ham bone in a kosher household.

"I don't want any soup," he said at dinner that night.

"We all start with soup." His father ladled him a bowl of cold borscht.

Norman joined the army. When he came home, he could not make a relationship with a woman stick, though he tried with a mother who had two children.

After he told the family he was gay, he moved to San Francisco and contracted AIDS. Sick with the disease and alone, he forgot his mother's reaction to his homosexuality. He moved back to the city where she lived and didn't talk to him.

Then one day, putting on flip flops that made his toes look like cloven hooves, he remembered again how he'd been a ham bone in a kosher home. He thought of the inkwell landing on the sidewalk that day, the sound of the glass shattering, its ink spreading stupid as soup. Did his action bring a *brokh*? He didn't believe in curses. *Nor gott vast*? Yes, should God only know.

In Between

When my morning coffee grows cold, I place
my mug in the microwave hoping for the best,
but this second chance has neither the rush
of the newly dripped nor the settled
quiet of later cold. It is a biting argument
toned down, a dismissive shrug of the shoulders.

The Lake between Us

I am bound to the ground, calculating distances
in the streets of towns and villages.

Oh, you who are ever the one not worried,
seem a mighty lifting into air.

This life of ours is one of contradiction,
a boat drifting around an anchor.

Not one time but so many, not many but an infinity.
Yet. And yet.

If You Are a Mother, If You Are a Daughter

I remember it was in October they came to get me.
My mother started to cry, "Her? She's just a little
girl! You can't take her." My mother put her best
shawl on me.

> — Juanita Cruz Blue Spruce,
> Ohkay Owingeh Pueblo,
> New Mexico 1915

If you are a mother, if you are a daughter,
you understand what that shawl meant when there
was nothing else from home to travel with you
but your mother's tears on this wool.

If you are a mother, if you are a daughter,
you understand what your grandmother's ring meant,
given to her by her mother, should she need it
for bribes and money running from pogroms.

If you are a mother, if you are a daughter,
you understand the miles of journey asylum seekers
make now in tee-shirts, in flipflops, nothing to give
their children but fortitude and the hope of living.

If you are a mother, if you are a daughter,
you understand the heartbreak of the little boy alone
on a beach when his parents drowned under a capsized
boat trying to escape from starving in a war zone.

If you are a mother, if you are a daughter,
you understand the fear and fury of children taken
from their parents at our border, dirty and wet,
looking up at armed agents' eyes.

If you are a mother, if you are a daughter,
understand your family could be next for whatever
reason misfortune knocks at your door. Imagine
no way to protect your children and nothing to give.

Love in a Time of Computer Geeks

A news report from Mexico puts me in mind
of Cozumel, of hailing one of the cabs
that haul tourists to the beach.

My husband sits again in front of his computer
reading binary code and packets, so I
imagine him wrapped in philodendrons.

They are epiphytes, I've learned, that grow
along the jungle tree bark. I hear again
a crescendo of tropical birds

and change into the bathing suit
I wore to snorkel among the colorful fish
at Chankanaab State Park.

This time, since he is a plant, I'll be a hawk
unraveling miles of fiberoptic cable
across the very blue sky.

In Winter

After work, under the streetlamp's
fuzzy light my father shoveled snow
from our sidewalk, steps, and driveway.

He refused to wear a hat, even after
hanging up his executive clothes,
even as his hair turned the color
of his morning coffee with cream.

"Bert! Bert! Be careful!" Mother called,
window raised, flakes blowing in,
as we two daughters emptied
packets of Swiss Miss into cups.

She worried he'd have a heart attack,
excitement of their formal parties and travels
ruined, the comfort of his income gone.

That isn't fair, of course, because she loved him,
but it is true that in those times,
a husband was everything.

The three of us stayed watching
through the window while the kettle whistled.
We wouldn't add water until he was done.

Huntress

Have you ever seen a predator
more wonderful than the great horned owl,
shaggy tufts atop her head?

Have you ever seen her head
swiveling a bit as she looks you over,
homegirl making her point?

And her point as she perches on a snag,
her eyes wide and large as our own,
is that she can swallow whatever

she eats whole and doesn't have to digest
what isn't digestible but throws it back up,
fur and feathers and bones.

How It Is

I.

A solar flare is expected in this century
to wipe out earth's electrical systems;
it will take years to get things running again.
Island nations will vanish as oceans rise;
bananas will go extinct.

II.

A bone discovered in southwest China
indicates another human species lived
beside us fourteen thousand years ago.

III.

My husband reads aloud from a story:
"People sleep peacefully in their beds at night
only because rough men stand ready
to do violence on their behalf."

IV.

A friend installed communication
satellites in war-torn countries. He said,
"The veneer of civilization is very thin."

At Ocean Shores My Husband Sings to the Sea

"It's a wonderful world," he croons to the waves
as if in their own tenacious rhythm, they need
reminding of nearby grasses, bluffs, and forest.

And too depressed by the news to read
papers, he sings over the hard-packed sand,
"I see skies of blue and clouds of white."

I walk downwind hoping he'll hold on to that.
It is he who told me the sparkle of sand diamonds
is light struggling to get out.

Opportunist

This morning, fur and feces in the trap
my husband bought on the advice
of a clerk at the hardware store.

Could the mouse have approached,
only the edge of its face touching
before the smell of glue overpowered
the peanut pieces sprinkled in the center?

Did the mouse move to the other side, hang
its behind over that edge and leave us
a note, shit a meaningful goodbye?

A Work-Around to Believe In

After Denise Champion's Painting Storm Coming

There may always be a storm coming,
but there are not always storms.

There may not always be a horizon,
but there is always something we can reach for.

Fields may not always be green,
but there are seeds in the fallow.

Burst of Hope

That when his snowboard's edge caught
on the day's icy slope and threw him
airborne toward the inevitable tree, my son
saw his soul spark over white clouds,
his sweet spirit rising beyond the land.

Four

No matter how deep my sleep I shall hear you…
— Eugene O'Neill

Dear Seth,

You would be forty-two today, and I am touring in Italy under the first cloudy sky of my two-week trip. Under the greying sky of Burano, I try to look at my surroundings through your eyes: houses, red, blue, yellow, green, pink, terracotta, with geraniums, begonias and petunias adding more color from pots on outdoor windowsills. Skiffs and small motorboats tied along the many canals lend reflections to the still water.

Wooden shutters cover windows; draperies hang over front doors to keep out heat and let in the breezes. Some of the structures have separate small, single-story buildings connected to them, acting it seems to this foreigner as entrances and exits.

I walk the pedestrian-only cobbled streets beyond lace shops, *osterias*, and gelato windows open every day for the boatloads of tourists who arrive each hour. I continue past an elementary school and stand by the young students' vegetable garden.

This is what I think of:

The marble cheese board and cutter you and Emily brought home from Italy the year as young children you traveled there with your father.

Your fleeting idea to postpone becoming an architect so you could open a brewery restaurant with friends on an island in the Caribbean.

The ice cream cones we bought at The Elevated, my town's one-story sweets shop, named years ago when the building had a second story and the town's first elevator.

You at four, your overalls' pockets full of snails and twigs.

I see a red kayak and think of your wooden one stored now in the crawl space under the house, your patience and attention to detail.

Before I turn to retrace my steps for the ferry back to Venice, I puzzle at a tall brick bell tower, somehow comfortable even after its fifteen-story axis has leaned six feet because of land subsidence, the term, I learn, for earth settling beneath the load of a built structure.

Andrea Tirali designed this tower in the early seventeen hundreds, getting away from the frills of the Baroque, predicting the Neoclassical in architecture. You would have marveled at the restraint in the design and at the very survival of the tower despite its lean. I like to think of you here with me, explaining how the tower can stand.

I board the boat away from the quiet I've found on the back streets of Burano and fifty minutes later begin to hear its gears grind as it slows for the many "bus stops" that float like barges along Venice's Grand Canal. I feel the jerk of it broadsiding each station where passengers disembark.

And with each teetering of my body, I think how structures can stand where there is great subsidence of soil, how a mother can grieve her son and at the same time continue with his life alongside hers, allow colors and sensations to keep him alive.

Love, as always,

Mom

At the Alsi Motel, Waldport, Oregon

I walk to the motel desk to find the laundry
when, in the profile of a young man
talking to the clerk, I see my son Seth,
now twenty years dead.

I see him in the round cut of this man's
curly hair and in the short beard that meets
that hair, in the shape of his fingers and his shoulders
rounding, as a leftie, he leans in to sign the motel's form.

And how was that for you? my husband asks
when I tell him. Are there any words for the moment
that took my breath away, the back of that curly hair
exactly like my son's when he was in college?

Tears usher in those words the next day.

Why isn't it my son checking in with a friend
for respite from the backpacking he loved?
Why isn't it my son sitting on a log
gazing at seals sunbathing on the sand bar
across the way, watching two blue herons fishing?

The moment I saw that curly sun-tinted hair
at the back of that young man's head,
what did I feel? Desire. I wanted him to turn
around and hug me happy to be saying
Mom, Mom.

Epiphany at Creek Trail Loop, North Cascades

Along the trail of western hemlock
and red cedar, I read the forest service
signs and learn the caddis fly glues together
a house of pebbles from the stream bed
where it hatched, then drags the house along,
feeding until it becomes a pupa with wings, then sheds
the stones protective as they were and flies.

When Doris Told Us about Brittlebush

I didn't mourn its yellow blossoms gone from stalks
still rising high above the plant's leaves.

I didn't wonder at the name's sound
broken in the middle like twigs snapped in my hand
but seeming whole like the beat of a drum.

I didn't think about the color grey of its leaves
offering protection from the desert sun or the fuzz
there that directs the warm dry winds away.

I was admiring our elderly guide, winter wind
and rain traveling through her hair, a design in it
like the imprint of one agave leaf upon another.

Wrapping Coins Accumulated
in an Aluminum Camping Pot

As I counted quarters into piles of ten, nickels and dimes,
then pennies, I heard the sound of you, Dad, emptying
your pockets at the highboy dresser in the bedroom
you shared with Mom and pictured myself
at the gold-flecked Formica table in our New Jersey
apartment learning to use the bank's paper wrappers.

We were counting coins from a ceramic bank
you'd filled for years. It was bright red
and a couple of feet tall. How like you, I realize, to have
not a pig, but something familiar as growing up in Brooklyn.
I heard again the drop of coins into the slot
at the top of your bank, my old question, "Is it filled yet?"

There was no plug at the bottom. You had to hammer it open.
It was fun to watch you shatter it, destroying something
instead of maintaining it with the care usual for you.
To start each roll, I learned to set the first coin
flat against my forefinger slipped inside,
and how like a Chinese finger trap it seemed
when I had to get my finger out.

This morning as I felt the weight of those filled wrappers,
I heard your words, *loose change, small change,*
no small potatoes. I had made a call to heaven standing
there at my table remembering listening to bagpipe music
on a vinyl record you bought from the A&P sale bin, teaching
me that change equals dollars and bargains
can expand horizons.

When Kurt woke up and saw the wrapped coins,
he said he'd read
the chances of winning the lottery are less than the chance
of dropping a penny from the top of the Empire State Building
into a cup placed on the sidewalk. I imagine not one coin,
but a skyscraper full of them, the silvery sound
of a young me and a young you and a table full of wealth.

As I Remember It

For My Sister

You wowed us with the horse's neigh
you taught yourself to imitate so well that neighbors
thought we kept one in our house.

On our bedroom wall, too, a painting of a charcoal-
colored horse on a pink background, treasure
our parents bought for you because you loved it.

How steady that love of yours, even with anger
at my unfulfilled promises to play Monopoly,
my refusal to allow you to wear a favorite hair bow.

Then you fell in love with Peggy Lee's voice.
"Everybody's got the fever," again and again
from the phonograph in our small room.

And there was the black hole of sad notes
you'd poked, I would learn, into the open seam
no one saw in the neck of your stuffed panda.

While the Artist Paints Fire, a Memory

My friend Eta cried as we stood in the courtyard
watching flames leap from her apartment
building's windows, felt the heat on our faces
as firemen in helmets the size of burls
on the city elms pulled heavy hoses from trucks.
I smelled the smoke in her clothes all that school year
until she outgrew them. How small my dirty
footprints on my mother's white carpet.

High School

Earning dollars mixing malteds
called *Awful Awfuls* lured me
from Saturday's drill team,
where I shouted and marched
in white cardigan and maroon skirt
that touched just above the knee.

I trained my shoulders to align
with shoulders next to mine,
wore boots and raised them
a standard distance from the ground.

Now in starched hat and small round apron,
I serve them up — *Awfully Big, Awfully Good!*
Drink three and the fourth is free!
Bloated showmanship and vomit
in the bathrooms.

I stand behind the soda counter
imagining a stride I'd call my own.

Hummingbird, Female

The female hummingbird builds her nest
with threads from a spider's web, knows how to ensure
it can expand as her young grow as big as she
two weeks after they hatch.

She'll tie what she's built to a branch, line it with grass
and seed pod down, camouflage it with lichen,
while the male she mated with is out finding another
woman to fertilize. That is his job.

She works body and tail to hollow a place for her eggs,
and after babies hatch, to find fruit flies to feed them.
All of this at eighty wing-beats a second and still she must visit
her one thousand flowers a day before restful torpor
    in night's cool air.

How the males intrigue us with brilliant gold and purple
at the back of their heads, even black handlebar mustaches
    on some.
How we talk of their splendor while the grey-green female,
with only a faint russet on her chest, births two broods a season.

May to December before she flies to warmer climes
she fattens herself up for her coming labor,
while the males leave on their journey north two weeks

before she will, their job to find a territory
free of other males and protect it, then to dance for the females
enticing them to mate and get to work.

Fall Fog Has Settled Again over Discovery Bay

Under the low clouds, I wish for summer and clear skies,
an early morning stroll through the garden ripe with peas,
raspberries, laughter of my visiting grandsons
who order "pancakes as big as the plate."

Out in the chilly, damp air, a cucumber hides beneath
leaves, a patty pan squash might yet ripen.
Amidst the curves of the vegetables, I see again
my grandsons' feet in brand new Crocs.

The older boy packed tomatoes he picked.
His younger brother drew a blue face on our garden gate.
The older one ate the ripe strawberries;
the younger one lay in bed, our cat sleeping at his feet.

I recollect the boys' tan bodies as they ran around stacked
cottage blocks pulling kale leaves to mark each lap they ran.
A therapist told me that wish is a child's word.
I toast to memories still fresh and young.

With My Mother

Each time we walk through the grocery's
automatic sliding doors, my mother
stops just inside the store where the vinyl
entrance mat ends. People drift around us
as if we are rocks in a stream bed
and she wobbles a little bit as she checks
her purse for items we already made sure
she brought: money, a credit card,
reading glasses, vehicle handicap plaque
we hadn't had to use this time for parking.
To the right is a cart I grab for her, its bar
something to help her keep steady.
As she begins to push, I remember
the diving board edges of my childhood,
my own hesitation before bouncing up
to plunge in and meet the fearsome waters.

Spring Equinox

For Judith Kitchen

I washed a winter's worth of collard greens,
tore their leaves from stems and veins, steamed
the greens in broth, added red pepper flakes,
cayenne, too, then ate the fans I'd frayed
and mixed with rice and beans.
I triple-washed the beets, separating greens
from bulbous roots. Roasted and boiled,
they helped me pull away from winter,
start remembering it's spring.

The peas go in, the onion sets, more fava beans,
soon cauliflower and tomatoes, the orange,
yellow, green, and maybe striped as well.
I pluck last year's shriveled figs, born too late
to ripen on our maturing tree, toss them behind
our fence with prayers that figs might sweeten
sooner now that years are moving faster toward an end
that I refuse to really see, though I know how fast
the growing and faster still we eat.

From My Window, June Sunset

Cedar and fir trees at the edge of the bay are an audience
in front row seats. They wear shawls, have colicky hair,
but from my seat in the back, I can see between them
to the orange sky, bright against a coming cloud cover
if I gaze over the heads of salal and Oregon grape.
Evening arrives with birdsong, the soft croaking of frogs.
It's an orchestra for the sky's choreography. I watch. I listen.
I eat a late dinner, savoring the sweetness of blueberries
still warm from a day's bright sun.

A Personal Archeology

What happened?
That day my sister learned about plaque buildup on her teeth,
and it plagued her. We lingered at the dinette table, the two
of us junior high school-aged, hands touching gold-flecked
Formica only feet from the kitchen sink with its stainless steel-
tiled backsplash, my mother's mark of distinction, my father's
weekend project in our sixties split level home in New Jersey.

I don't know where our parents had gone or which of us that
night was to wash and which to dry. There were grapes from
dessert still on the table and I thought somehow to advise my
sister to cut a grape and rub its insides over her teeth.

"Will it work?" she asked as she did it.

"I don't know. I just thought of it." I shrugged.

She frowned, said my name with that familiar gurgle at the la
part, as if it were ga, making me feel I was always
clogging pipes.

So what?
I felt mean, like I had tried to trick her, but really it was just an
idea, something I thought somehow might work, those grapes
right there in front of us.

Did you leave?
Well, yes. I walked toward the sink.

And then what?
Years later, I read that grape seed extract is helpful in fighting
dental plaque. But it would go on like this, her disgust making
me sorry.

Do you know where you are from?
I was born in Richmond, Virginia, at the Stuart Circle Hospital,
perhaps during a thunderstorm of Gothic proportions, like
when I visited the building recently and lightning struck the
bronze statue of Jeb Stuart in the center of the circle.

What did you think at the hospital?
I wondered where a declaration of independence lived in me,
what its weight was and had been.

What of today?
My tall paper coffee cup sits on the table before me, its formal
white torso topped by a black derby; its cummerbund of brown
paper proclaiming "Hot Beverage" around what I might call
its waist.

"Elegant" arrives on my tongue. Shall I write smoking jackets
of silk and sparkles on ball gowns, hot hope and permission to
behave jauntily and intoxicated, take the world into my lungs,
take it all in and dance?

Your parents: What did they say?
How can you?
You are wrong to feel that way! You will kill your father if you
do. Take care of your mother.

What did your sister say?
It's my turn.
Why did they give it to you? Why are you always first?

What do you see now?
In the center of my backyard, a field of orange calendula and the tall leaves of Shasta daisies. At the edges of my backyard, purple foxglove, sword ferns, Oregon grape.

What do you write?
He never said that was a good idea, embarking on becoming a poet. "What was I going to do?" he asked. From my first collection: my father snoring locomotives, our aspiring front lawn. When he was diagnosed with Parkinson's, I wrote about hushing the tremors in one arm with the other, about holding himself as his parents between their feuds had never held him.

What was I going to do?
What I always do.

Precocial, Tucson Desert Museum

I stand shaky and wet on legs I have not stood
on before but must move quickly or be caught
by coyote, eagle, or hawk.

I look for crags in high rocks, spots
of shade under jojoba trees, and bighorn sheep
to teach me the way up bluffs.

I learn the false prosperity in tarantulas'
four hundred eggs, think it sadness
in the deers' eyes glossed from an extra membrane.

I stand guard for those who travel into burrows
for food, and then like an ocelot, drape
myself over the octopus agave's untoothed leaves.

I watch from there, but when I have to, I leap
subtle among life's brush, hide in heavier vegetation
until in moonlight it is safe to follow my dreams.

Solar Eclipse, August 21, 2017, Corvallis, Oregon

Oh and *oh*, tango of moon's shadow and sun,
celestial bodies moving to closed embrace

until all we see is sun's corona,
safe then to take off our glasses, witness

the silver of this circumference.
I did not expect my eyes to fill with tears

when the two turned wholly into one.
I am surprised by tears again

when moon releases her partner into corte
and sun takes to lighting the sky.

In Gargnano, Italy

> *I lie in bed watching the sunrise. The lake lies dim and*
> *milky, the mountains are dark blue at the back, while*
> *over them the sky gushes and glistens with light.*
> — D. H. Lawrence

On the shores of Lake Garda, I bow before the cypress trees'
columnar height, the Roman ruins among the *limonetos*.
I see the Alps where D.H. Lawrence walked with Frieda,
stand near the house they lived in, cappuccino in the morning,
afternoon espresso, grappa at night.

In the lake, sardines, *lavaret*, pike and perch, the slip of moss
on cold rocks, chill of bathing in the clear Alpine
    spring-fed water,
three ducks and a swan on a pebbled beach, a father who throws
his fishing net over the stone wall of a restaurant's terrace
while his three children watch for their dinner.

I breathe deeply, happy to relinquish my old grievances
with every spoonful of gelato, pistachio, fig, red pomegranates
ripening on their vines over a villa's iron fence,
olive trees close by and ready for harvest. I want
    to walk the cobbled
street here forever where sail boats and skiffs moor
    so close to shore.

Van Gogh Morning

In a vase on my table, eight sunflowers,
a gift from a friend's yard. She says she lets
the crop go to seed each year to feed the birds
and the undigested plentifully spread and sprout in summer.
And here they are, these flowers sturdy on the necks
    of their stems,
my room overcome with their fancy yellow collars,
their searching brown eyes.

Hawaii Haiku

Slatted blinds rocking
Before an open window
Breeze's lullaby

Ceiling fan blades swirl
Reflection in my sunglasses
Festival surprise

For You Today

For Kim Krahn

May angels smooth sweet-scented lotion
on your elbow's rough patches, braid your hair.
Listen while they sing their song of weaving.

Don't move away too soon; don't shake
your head in no's. Remember a lover's words to you.
Tell clouds they wear their costumes well.

Look at sunlight dappling water, the hundreds of florets
inside each sunflower, the way your horse's hooves
lift above the earth before they thunder.

On Aging

I tell my husband I want an updated stove,
refrigerator, and dishwasher for the dozen
years I have before my eighties.

I want five-year warranties, renewable
for another three, whatever time
good credit buys.

I say yes to new technologies' beeps,
message texts, and rapid boils,
redesigns for better functioning.

I want sophisticated sensors to bless
what I freeze, wash, and heat.
I will feel younger in their embrace.

Evening Song

In the quiet you hear the birdsong
that drove you once so quickly from the family
dinner table to play in hours left of daylight,
hit the penny on the head, pink rubber ball you held
a yard from where the penny lay on your front sidewalk
or other nights hopped big squares your friends had chalked,
while parents chatted, happy on porch steps.

Sometimes if the light lasted you rode your bike
to a seemingly far field, empty and full of possibility,
then rode back at twilight to the comforting glow
of parents' cigarettes in the coming dark.

This evening you walk deserted streets accompanied
by music of those birds, so close, so far away, and notice
the mugo pines in neighbors' front yards, how thick, dark
green this year's spring candles have become, pointing
as they do toward the magnificent and timeless sky.

There Is a Street

There is a street I walk down past old
homes substantial and strong, though porch
railings and window trims are rotting,
maybe the boards too where wood siding
meets their rough cement foundations.

There's always a side entrance to a basement,
perhaps a student apartment now, lawns
dotted with crab grass, and often rooms added
in remodels that match the vintage.

I breathe easy in the presence of old homes, tonic
of memories, feel kinship with their residents,
who must add rooms for more living
despite what creaks and sags.

And So to Sleep

Sometimes I go to sleep with my heart full of sadness,
a student's poem that day about a bicycling daughter
killed by a bus as it made a turn, someone's essay
about losing her son to a strep infection that went to his heart,
another's about grieving the mother she had and the one
she never had because of bipolar disorder.

Sometimes my mind is full of lines from a poem
I am happy to have written, even if I am unsure it is finished.
Other times a busy brain can't stop making lists of all
I forgot to do that day, emails to answer buried now
under stacks of new email, phone calls promised and not made,
forms still to be filled out, bills to be paid.

Sometimes if I have taken the time to weed my garden I see
behind closed eyes the intricate designs of unwanted plants
as if I am still reaching for them. Somehow, I drift off to sleep
until the light of a full moon awakens me or a random
robo call causes my phone to ring at an hour no one
would call unless it was an emergency, which is why I keep
my phone on overnight as I worry that my mother,
who is in her nineties, will need something.

Sometimes I sleep till nine AM despite the dawn and early
sunlight or get up at four or five or six, the pleasure of not
having to rush into the day; whatever has happened overnight
no longer as disconcerting as when I had to be up and driving
to teach eight AM university classes.

Sometimes boiling water for drip coffee, I peruse the extra
list I scribbled after walking from bed to the dining room,
restless about what I might forget by morning.
Sometimes I turn to the news, assuring myself the world
is still there despite its greed and confusion.

Sometimes I walk out into my garden to see seedlings
sprouting or fruit beginning to form on the Asian pear trees,
the figs rounding themselves. I think of how I planted
a seed mix along the outside of my garden fence to grow
flowers that deer, rodents and raccoons avoid. My botanist
neighbor frowned. There were weeds in the mix.

Sometimes, I look for words that keep away writing
I want to grow, call them "weed words" as I uproot them.
How they have pioneered the soil, made it rich
and ready to receive what I must write.

The Spill

For Stan Rubin

For some reason, he never stopped waving his hands
as he spoke, even if the stemware glass of red wine
was an eighth of an inch from his fingers.

You'd think he had the spatial sense of a cat
or the lightest of touches like a hummingbird
sipping nectar from a blossom, never injuring it.

But he grew more animated and eventually
tipped the glass over, the red liquid splayed on my jeans
where no one could see it,

the way they couldn't see his grief right now,
second Christmas eve since his wife died,
the space between his hands and the fallen glass
larger than when it stood upright,

as if he pushed his grief away to make
space for mourner's guilt at having not been
enough to keep her alive, and these days, for finding
cheer wherever he could.

When he apologized for the spill, I brushed my hands
over the slight damp on my lap, and I knew I would write:
grief is not feline-subtle, but hopefully it has wings.

I wake to snow mittens at the tips of pines, cedar branches
dressed up in white sleeves, the asphalt of our streets
covered with inches of plush carpeting.

It's a Zen dream, Discovery Bay and the December
sky wearing matching robes of warm grey, seagulls
circling as if to unify heaven and earth.

I offer thanks for the peace of this morning,
for every morning we might breathe
newly freshened air.

Bereaved, I Turn to Gardening

Grief is an obligation to the life one has been
awarded, an obligation to life to make more life.
— Martin Prechtel

Before I can eat, I must prepare; before I prepare,
I must harvest; before I harvest, I must plant;
before I plant, I must enrich soil with minerals

contributed by other plants, plants I leave there
so their roots make nitrogen for seeds to plant again,
watered, given space, harvested not too early, not too late,

and I keep these seeds, at least some of them,
protected from the hungry squirrels of attachment,
away from mold that forms on memories.

I eat what I have grown, what I harvest, and what I chop,
what I cook to break down so I can metabolize
this world and feed yours, my deceased and beloved son.

Now

To Seth on his birthday, October 1, 2019

I read time now like a book front to back or back to front,
midsection first, or by random pages.
Changing it up spins your life longer somehow
and though I know the ending can never be rewritten,
I savor who you were and who you will always be,
write catching-ups and checking-ins to create more
love for me to feel in the only present possible.

So in this season come round again in the rush of fall
wind and thickening clouds of winter, I can
still imagine sun and a wife and children paddling
with you along the shores of Discovery Bay,
gleaming wood of the kayaks visible as they move
farther and farther from where I stand
holding them dear even as I must let them go.

Acknowledgments

Some of the poems in *Since Then* have appeared in the following journals:

"At a Window by a Ravine," "How It Is," and "The Lake Between Us" in *Cathexis Northwest Press*, November 1, 2020.

"Who Lives on the Other Side" in *Griffel*, December 2020.

"Pantoum from Northern Jutland" in *The Lake*, June 2020.

"Huntress" in *The Madrona Project: Human Communities in Wild Places*, Volume II, Number 2, January 2022, Empty Bowl Press.

"The Old Neighborhood in Winter, a Villanelle" in *Showbear Family Circus*, December 11, 2020.

"To the Fiancée Who Fled Three Weeks Before the Wedding Date" was commissioned for *Signs of Life Literary and Art Journal*, Facèré Jewelry Art Gallery, Seattle, Washington, 2014.

"Left" in *Unstamatic*, April 2020.

"Everyday Excitement," "Fall Fog Has Settled Again Over Discovery Bay," "From My Window, June Sunset," and "Spring Equinox" in *Wording the Land Poetry Collection 2019*, sponsored by the Jefferson County Farmers Markets Organization in partnership with Finnriver Farm and Cidery in Port Townsend, Washington. "Spring Equinox" was also previously featured in the *Poem Inspired, 2016: Celebrating Ten Years of the Northwind Reading Series*.

About the Author

Photo by Emily Menon Bender

Sheila Bender co-founded WritingItReal.com in 2002 with her husband Kurt VanderSluis as a website dedicated to facilitating writing from personal experience. Over the years as the internet grew, the venue grew to include an array of online and Zoom classes as well as publications of anthologies. For five-plus years, Sheila produced the KPTZ FM radio program "In Conversation: Discussions on Writing and the Writing Life." She has taught for Centrum Foundation's Port Townsend Writer's Workshop as well as writers' conferences and centers, colleges, and universities across the West and Southwest, including a stint as Distinguished Guest Lecturer for Seattle University. She lives in Port Townsend, Washington, where she nurtures a big vegetable garden and dreams and writes overlooking Discovery Bay.

The text of *Since Then* is set in Minion Pro, with the titles in Gil Sans. The book was printed on 70-lb. offset white Boise paper at Bookmobile in Minneapolis, Minnesota.